contents

I0411700

introduction

According to the most recent U.S. Census figures, there are over 17 million Asian American and Pacific Islanders (AAPIs) in the United States today. As one of the most culturally and linguistically diverse groups in the country, AAPIs trace their heritage to over 30 different countries and ethnic groups and speak over 100 languages and dialects. From 2000 to 2010, Asian Americans experienced a 43 percent increase and Native Hawaiians and Pacific Islanders experienced a 30 percent increase in population.

To help understand what these changing demographics mean for the federal government, President Obama reauthorized the White House Initiative on AAPIs on Oct. 14, 2009, to improve the quality of life of AAPIs by better connecting them with federally available programs and protections. Although AAPIs have helped build a strong and vibrant U.S., many still face linguistic isolation, poverty, immigration issues, and other barriers to achieving their full potential.

This *Guide to Federal Agency Resources* is an easy-to-use navigational tool on federal funding, programs, and resources. It is by no means comprehensive, but it is meant to provide a brief snapshot of federal resources available to assist organizations and individuals seeking to improve the quality of life of AAPIs. Within this guide, individuals and organizations can find such information as grant opportunities for nonprofit organizations, loan programs to help start a business, federal resources for food and housing for low-income individuals, and health-care programs for veterans.

For each federal entity highlighted, the first section provides a short description of online search engines for federal government grants. Each subsequent section provides an overview of the federal agency, selected services and programs that agency offers, and links to additional resources. This guide also includes *10 Grantee Spotlights*, featuring organizations and individuals who have successfully navigated the federal grant application process and can offer advice, by example, to prospective applicants.

"As a small grassroots organization with little experience in applying for federal grants and limited knowledge of the technical language used in grant applications, the process was a bit scary at first ... My advice for those interested in this program is to seek out support and guidance from the community and local decision makers."

—EPA Grantee, Seattle, Wash., September, 2011.

searching for federal assistance and grants

Grants administered by federal agencies differ by eligibility requirements, award amount, application process, and timing. Two online resources can help you determine what types of funding are available and how to apply for that funding.

Grants.gov is the primary source of information and mode of submitting applications for federal grants and awards of financial assistance, administered through 1,000 programs and 26 federal grant-making agencies to recipients carrying out a public purpose of support or stimulation. In FY2009, Grants.gov received over 300,000 application submissions. Users must complete the Grants.gov registration process, which requires organizations to obtain a Data Universal Number System (DUNS) number and to register with the Central Contractor Registry (CCR). There is a user guide available, and for general questions, call: 1-800-518-4726 or email support@grants.gov. Note: The registration process takes approximately three to five business days.

Catalog of Federal Domestic Assistance (CFDA) is a governmentwide compendium of all federal programs available to state and local governments; domestic public, quasi-public, and private profit and nonprofit organizations and institutions; specialized groups; and individuals. Organizations may utilize the CFDA to identify programs and information on federal financial and nonfinancial assistance; however, only government agencies can apply for grants on the CFDA website directly. There is a user guide available, and individuals may purchase the CFDA by contacting the U.S. Superintendent of Documents at 1-866-512-1800 or the U.S. Government Printing Office's online bookstore. For assistance using the CFDA website, you may contact the Federal Service Desk or call 1-866-606-8220.

The Federal Register is the official daily publication of the federal government and provides Notices of Funds Available (NOFA). The U.S. Government Printing Office's *Federal Register* database makes it easy to search for updates and information on the most recent grant and award opportunities.

Grantee Spotlight: Monsoon United Asian Women of Iowa; Des Moines, Iowa
Federal Program: Culturally and Linguistically Specific Services for Victims Program; DOJ, OVW

Monsoon was formed in 2003 as a culturally specific advocacy group under the auspices of the Iowa Coalition Against Sexual Assault. The group aims to provide services to Asian victims and survivors of domestic violence and sexual assault in Iowa, which include violence prevention, community outreach, engaging youths to stop violence against women and girls, and providing direct services to survivors and victims of domestic violence and sexual assault.

Executive Director and Cofounder Mira Yusef explains her experience applying for Grants to Enhance Culturally and Linguistically Specific Services for Victims of Domestic Violence, Dating Violence, Sexual Assault and Stalking Program (CLSSP), and Sexual Assault Services Program—Grants to Culturally Specific Programs (SASP-CLSP).

We heard about these grants through two national advocacy organizations, the Asian Pacific Islander Institute on Domestic Violence and the National Organization of Sisters of Color Ending Sexual Assault. With these grants, we were able to hire a full-time Mobile Multilingual Advocate Coordinator, two part-time Mobile Multilingual Advocates based in satellite locations, a part-time Community Outreach Coordinator, two Advocacy Interns and 10-20 on-call Mobile Multilingual Advocates located throughout Iowa to facilitate a statewide effort. The SASP-CLSP is directed towards victims across their lifespan, with specific attention to culture and generation. Our "Unburdening Our Mothers Oral History Project," is intended to dismantle the shroud of silence hanging over sexual assault among API elders. To further encourage discourse about sexual assault within younger generations, up to 30 youth peer-to-peer counselors and outreach staff will be hired and trained over three years.

OVW provides valuable technical assistance to prospective grantees throughout the application process. OVW hosts calls to assist through the process, and the grant manager is also available to provide assistance if needed. The most difficult part of the application process was obtaining the DUNS number. I actually enjoyed the process, but I have to say, I may be an aberration!

For those who would like to apply for this grant, I advise you to consult with other organizations for best practice advice, and shape them to fit your community's needs. Don't be discouraged and keep on writing. If you are not successful, try again!

For more information on OVW programs, visit here.

resources by federal department

U.S. Department of Agriculture (USDA)

How it can assist AAPIs

The USDA is a federal agency with a broad range of responsibilities including: serving the hungry, supporting development in rural communities, preserving the environment through conservation programs, monitoring food safety, and supporting American farmers, ranchers, and consumers.

Food and Nutrition Services programs help one in every five Americans get the nutrition they need. USDA relies on state governments and local organizations to help get food to low-income households. Some of the most relevant programs to AAPI communities include:

The Supplemental Nutrition Assistance Program (SNAP) helps low-income individuals and families buy the food they need for good health. On the SNAP website you'll find an Eligibility Pre-Screening Tool, which can help determine if you may be eligible to receive SNAP benefits, and a Community Partner Outreach Toolkit, which is full of great resources and how-tos.

The Senior Farmers' Market Nutrition Program awards grants to states, U.S. territories, and federally recognized Indian tribal governments to provide low-income seniors with coupons that can be exchanged for certain foods at farmers' markets, roadside stands, and community-supported agriculture programs.

The National School Lunch Program is a federally assisted meal program operating in public and nonprofit private schools and residential child care institutions.

The Women, Infants and Children (WIC) supplemental nutrition program provides federal grants to states for supplemental foods, health care referrals, and nutrition education for low-income pregnant, breastfeeding, and non-breastfeeding postpartum women, and to infants and children up to age 5 who are found to be at nutritional risk. Currently, about 9 million individuals participate in this nutrition assistance program.

The Farm to School Initiative is an effort to connect schools (K–12) with regional or local farms to serve healthy meals using locally produced foods.

The 2007 Census of Agriculture shows that U.S. farmers and ranchers are becoming more diverse and that the number of Asian operators grew 40 percent from 2002, significantly outpacing the 7 percent increase in U.S. operators overall.

Direct grants for nonprofit organizations and loan opportunities from agencies within USDA are available. Eligibility varies, with some available to nonprofit organizations and local governments, and others for individuals and businesses. Organizations can apply directly for grants on the Grants.gov website (see more on Grants.gov on page 2).

The Community Food Projects Competitive Grant Program (CFP) funds nonprofit organizations to meet the food needs of low-income people by increasing their communities' capacities to provide enough food for its residents. To be considered competitive for a CFP grant, organizations should have experience in community food work, job training, and business development in low-income communities, and the application has a dollar-for-dollar matching requirement.

Applicants should also demonstrate a willingness to share information with researchers and other practitioners. Projects can be funded from one to three years.

The Risk Management Agency (RMA) Community Outreach and Assistance Partnership Program provides funds to organizations which offer risk management training to limited resource, socially disadvantaged, traditionally underserved (including women), and beginning farmers and ranchers. RMA staff work closely with grantees and help to implement the program activities. Funding amounts and educational topics change annually and new focus areas are announced in the Federal Register.

The Farmers Market Promotion Program grants are designed to increase marketing opportunities for farmers to sell directly to consumers through farmers' markets, community-supported agriculture (CSA) programs, retail markets, and other direct marketing initiatives. These grants can go to nonprofits, agricultural cooperatives or producer associations, local governments, economic development corporations, regional farmers' market authorities, public benefit corporations, and tribal governments. Visit the website to read the full application requirements, review previously-funded programs, and see two recently released tools to assist organizations with the grant-writing process: a pre-application guide and a presentation on grant-writing regarding this program.

The National Organic Program (NOP) regulates the well-known "USDA Organic" label and ensures that customers are buying what is promised with that label. For farmers, NOP regulates what is allowed and not allowed under the USDA Organic label, as well as provides technical assistance and cost sharing to receive official organic accreditation. The USDA strategic plan calls for a 25 percent increase in organic production by 2015.

The Rural Development Agency (RD) has various grant and loan programs to help develop housing, community facilities, and businesses in small towns and rural communities (with exact definition of "rural" varying depending on program). Organizations can apply directly for grants on the Grants.gov website (see more on Grants.gov on page 2), but there is a wealth of information and technical assistance at state and local RD offices, which should be your first stop. RD administers programs, including Value-Added Producer Grants, Rural Business Enterprise Grants, Rural Business Opportunity Grants, Rural Cooperative Development Grants, and Small Socially-Disadvantaged Producer Grants.

The Natural Resources Conservation Service has a leadership role in developing partnerships to help America's private landowners conserve their soil, water, and other natural resources. Certain programs also provide financial assistance for agricultural producers to rehabilitate farmland damaged by natural disasters and pests. For example, the Environmental Quality Incentives Program (EQIP) Organic Initiative provides technical and financial assistance and equipment to farmers transitioning to organic production. Local NRCS offices can help create a conservation plan that will preserve farmland, protect natural resources, and reduce soil erosion.

Civil rights protection and enforcement prohibits discrimination against USDA's customers on the bases of race, color, religion, sex, age, national origin, marital status, sexual orientation, familial status, disability, or because all or a part of an individual's income is derived from a public assistance program. To file a program discrimination complaint, you may visit the website, call 202-260-1026 or 1-866- 632-9992 (toll-free), send an email to CR-INFO@ascr.usda.gov, or write a letter to: U.S. Department of Agriculture, Director, Office of Adjudication, 1400 Independence Ave. S.W., Washington, DC 20250-9410.

Department of Commerce (DOC)

How it can assist AAPIs

The DOC works to improve economic conditions that foster entrepreneurship and innovation within the U.S. and create global competitiveness and opportunities. DOC has 12 bureaus that administer programs in areas that include foreign trade, technology, economic development, and environmental stewardship. DOC services provide economic data about U.S. companies, statistical details about neighborhoods, and patent and trademark protection for inventors and businesses.

With 1.5 million AAPI-owned businesses in the U.S. generating more than $507 billion dollars in sales and employing more than 2.8 million workers, success of AAPI-owned businesses is critical to the overall economy. Between 2002 and 2007, the number of U.S. businesses owned by Asian Americans increased by 40.4 percent, — more than twice the national rate.

— U.S. Census Bureau, Census Bureau Reports the Number of Asian-Owned Businesses Increased at More Than Twice the National Rate, April 2011.

The Minority Business Development Agency (MBDA) assists minority-owned businesses by providing companies with tools to access capital, contract opportunities, and business consultants through its network of nearly 50 minority business centers around the country that offer local experts who can help write business plans and marketing strategies; help locate capital and other funding resources; and provide technical assistance and financial planning to assure sufficient financing for business ventures. MBDA focuses on firms that generate $1 million or more in annual revenue. While MBDA will assist any business seeking help, it often will refer smaller businesses, especially those starting out, to the Small Business Administration (SBA) (for more on the SBA see page 34).

The Economic Development Administration (EDA) promotes the economic revitalization of distressed communities by providing grant-based investments that attract private capital and create higher-skill, higher-wage jobs. EDA fosters two key elements through its six regional offices: groundbreaking innovation by entrepreneurs, and regional collaboration between government entities, nonprofit organizations, education institutions, and Indian tribes. Among EDA's programs and investment priorities are:

- Economic Adjustment Assistance, EDA's most flexible program tool, provides funding to communities to develop strategic plans, deliver technical assistance, or establish or recapitalize revolving loan funds, to address critical economic development needs in the wake of severe disruptions to their economies.

- The University Center Economic Development program provides strategic investments to help institutions of higher education promote the regional ecosystem and facilitate collaboration among regional stakeholders to foster economic development

The exporting of goods and services has increasingly become a next step for many AAPI entrepreneurs wanting to expand their businesses. More than 95 percent of the world's consumers live outside U.S. borders, according to the International Trade Administration, which oversees Export.gov, and provides tools for small business owners on how to enter the exporting industry, including:

- An online assessment to help determine whether a business is ready to pursue international sales.

- A webinar on basic information on exporting, product readiness, market research, and how to best comply with foreign regulations.

AAPI business owners can get export help and counseling through the Export Assistance Centers available in more than 100 cities. The offices are staffed by trade professionals who provide counseling and services with an emphasis on small- and mid-sized businesses.

Businesses wanting to protect their inventions, brand names, or symbols identifying their goods and services can do so through the U.S. Patent and Trademark Office (USPTO).

- Each year, USPTO receives about 350,000 patent applications, most of them for utility patents. For information on the application process, visit: http://www.uspto.gov/patents/process or call: 1-800-786-9199.

- Trademarks include words, names, symbols, or devices used to identify the goods and services of one business from those produced or sold by others. The trademark database can be found at http://tess2.uspto.gov. The application can be filed online at http://www.uspto.gov/teas.

Along with the once-every-decade headcount, the U.S. Census Bureau conducts more than 100 monthly and annual surveys that gather data about housing, transportation, education, employment, veterans services, public health care, rural development, and the environment. Census data provides everything from a neighborhood's average home value, commute times, and residential diversity, to unemployment figures and statistics on health insurance coverage, to what foreign languages are spoken at home and in which cities. Among the more frequently used Census surveys:

- The annual American Community Survey measures demographic, social, and economic characteristics that help describe the way we live and where we work.

- The Census of Governments provides an overview of the lives of those whose livelihoods are supported by tax dollars—state and local government employees—and the financial state of the entities they work for.

- The Survey of Income and Program Participation collects data on incomes, employers, health-care costs, and such government programs as food assistance and subsidized housing.

- The Survey of Business Owners gathers data on the gender, ethnicity, race, and veteran status of the people running businesses in the United States.

Grantee Spotlight: Foxit Corporation, Fremont, Calif.
Federal Program: Minority Business Development Administration; DOC

With a limited command of English and even less understanding of U.S. small business financing, Eugene Y. Xiong came to the U.S. in 1994 from China and set out to achieve the American dream. The Minority Business Development Agency (MBDA) assisted Xiong's Foxit Corporation in becoming a multi-million-dollar company, which produces an alternative to Adobe for PDF users, with customers including Microsoft, Intel and Hewlett Packard. Mr. Xiong never heard of MBDA before his banker referred him to the MBDA's San Jose Business Center after failed attempts to obtain loans and other financing. He recalls the first question he asked MBDA: How much will this cost me? The answer: Nothing. Mr. Xiong remembers the assistance he received from MBDA to grow his successful business.

When we were tight on cash flow, MBDA helped us find the right banking service, and we got the right cash that we needed to grow our business. They have been constantly in contact with us and provide consulting and referral services. We also received information about the government procurement process.

I didn't know there were government services like this. I wish I had learned about this earlier. This is the kind of service that people need to know about. My advice to small, minority-owned businesses, like my own, is this: Do not hesitate in seeing what resources the government can offer you.

More about MBDA and its services can be found at http://www.mbda.gov.

Department of Education (ED)

How it can assist AAPIs

ED establishes and executes the president's education policy, implements laws enacted by Congress, and administers and coordinates federal assistance to education. ED's elementary and secondary programs annually serve more than 14,000 school districts and approximately 56 million students attending some 97,000 schools and 28,000 private schools. Its programs also provide grant, loan, and work-study assistance to approximately 11 million postsecondary students.

The Office of Elementary and Secondary Education (OESE) administers all programs for the country's elementary and secondary schools. Below are programs relevant to students and community organizations.

- 21st Century Community Learning Centers provide academic enrichment opportunities during nonschool hours for children, particularly students who attend high-poverty and low-performing schools. Formula grants are provided to state education agencies (SEAs) and are sub-granted to local education agencies (LEAs), nonprofit organizations, or other public or private entities.

- The Native Hawaiian Education Program promotes innovative programs and supplemental education services (including early education, literacy, and postsecondary programs) for Native Hawaiians. Nonprofit organizations are eligible to apply directly.

- The Education for Homeless Children and Youth Grants for state and local activities gather comprehensive information about homeless children and youths and provides grants to SEAs to ensure that homeless children have equal access to free and appropriate public education.

- The Teacher Incentive Fund supports development of performance-based teacher and principal compensation systems in high-need schools. SEAs, LEAs, and nonprofit organizations may apply.

- The Race to the Top awards SEAs that are leading the way with ambitious yet achievable plans for implementing coherent, compelling, and comprehensive education reform.

The Office of Postsecondary Education (OPE) administers over 60 programs that increase access to quality postsecondary education.

- The Alaska Native and Native Hawaiian Serving Institutions program and the Asian American and Native American Pacific Islander-Serving Institutions (AANAPISI) program helps eligible institutions of higher education (IHEs) increase their self-sufficiency and expand their capacity to serve low-income students by providing funds to improve and strengthen the academic quality, institutional management, and fiscal stability of eligible IHEs.

- The Fund for the Improvement of Postsecondary Education (FIPSE) supports innovative projects, reforms, and improvements in U.S. postsecondary education. Nonprofit organizations are eligible to apply directly.

- The College Access Challenge Grant Program helps low-income students succeed in postsecondary education by funding SEA programs to: provide information to students and families regarding postsecondary education and career preparation; promote financial literacy and debt management; conduct outreach activities; and other activities.

- Federal TRIO Programs include eight programs at IHEs and community organizations targeted to serve low-income individuals, first-generation college students, and individuals with disabilities to progress from middle school to postbaccalaureate programs. Programs include Talent Search, Upward Bound, and Student Support Services.

Federal Student Aid (FSA) administers grants, loans, and work-study assistance to postsecondary students. Students interested in any of these programs must complete the Free Application for Federal Student Aid (FAFSA).

- The Federal Pell Grant Program provides need-based grants to low-income undergraduate and certain post baccalaureate students to promote access to postsecondary education.

- Other Federal Student Aid grants including the Teacher Education Assistance for College and Higher Education Grants (TEACH) can be found here.

- The Federal Direct Student Loan Program provides loans directly to students for undergraduate and graduate studies, through participating postsecondary schools, with funds borrowed from the

U.S. Treasury. Direct Loans include subsidized and unsubsidized loans, PLUS loans for parents and graduate or professional degree students, and consolidation loans, which allow borrowers to combine federal education loan debt.

▪ Federal Work-Study programs provide part-time employment for students while they are enrolled in school. Students are paid directly for their work and schools are responsible for administering the program.

▪ The Stafford Loan Forgiveness Program for Teachers forgives up to a combined total of $17,500 in principal and interest on loans by individuals who teach full-time for five consecutive, complete academic years in certain elementary and secondary schools that serve low-income families. Students may also be eligible to defer or cancel loans.

The Office for Civil Rights (OCR) ensures equal access to education and promotes educational excellence through vigorous enforcement of civil rights. OCR serves students facing discrimination and the advocates and institutions promoting systemic solutions to civil rights problems. To file a complaint: You may contact an OCR enforcement office, call 1-800-421-3481, or use the online complaint form.

▪ ED, along with the departments of Defense, Justice, Health and Human Services, Agriculture, and the Interior form the Obama Administrations Inter-Agency Task Force on Bullying and launched both the *Stop Bullying Now Campaign* and http://www.bullyinginfo.org, a national database of effective anti-bullying programs.

Grantee Spotlight: South Seattle Community College; Seattle, Wash.
Federal Program: Asian American and Native American Pacific Islander Serving Institution (AANAPISI); ED

South Seattle Community College (South) is located in a diverse residential neighborhood in southwest Seattle. It is the lowest income area in the Pacific Northwest. AAPIs comprise the largest group of color on campus at 23 percent of the student population. However, less than 3 percent of the surrounding AAPI community is enrolled, with most students coming from other parts of the country.

In 2008, South's vice president of Student Services read about the AANAPISI program in a local newspaper. Subsequently, with the help of a Community Advisory Committee formed by South's president and an institutional development consultant, they submitted a successful application and became one of the first six recipients in the country to receive the AANAPISI designation and funding.

South's AANAPISI grant focused on breaking down the barriers to access, retention, and success of AAPI students. Strategies included the development of culturally relevant programs that acknowledge the importance of family; engaging students through pedagogically sensitive learning communities; providing role models and mentoring; providing resources to transition to college level course work, offering two new degree options, and the development of a virtual website of promising practices and resources to support the success of AAPIs in higher education.

For institutions of higher education interested in the AANAPISI program, South recommends finding a strong internal champion and enlisting a campus coordinator to pull together a team and information to develop the grant. Institutions should also get input from their AAPI community and work to debunk the Model Minority Myth. To learn more about South's AANAPISI program, visit http://www.aapiherc.southseattle.edu/.

Department of Energy (DOE)

How it can assist AAPIs

DOE advances science and technology in disciplines relevant to energy, the environment, and security.

DOE supports a wide range of basic and applied scientific research. For example, through the Office of Science, DOE offers research grants and contracts for universities, nonprofit organizations, for-profit commercial organizations, state and local governments, and unaffiliated individuals. The Advanced Research Projects Agency-Energy (ARPA-E) provides funding opportunities for the research and development of high-risk and high-reward advanced energy technologies. DOE also supports Science, Technology, Engineering, and Mathematics (STEM) education to recruit new K–12 teachers, enhance existing STEM teacher knowledge and skills, and provide greater STEM education for students.

Energy efficiency: DOE works with state governments to fund a network of community action agencies, nonprofit organizations, and local governments to provide weatherization information and services, including weatherization of low-income homes. Consumers can get tax credits for home energy efficiency improvements, residential renewable energy, and automobiles. DOE provides homeowners with energy saving tips in the Energy Savers booklet.

Loans and grants are available for small business innovation, training program development, energy efficient technology, lighting, and advanced energy manufacturing for industrial, commercial and residential energy efficiency purposes. Rebates and tax credits are also offered for energy-efficient businesses using renewable energy. The Loan Programs Office guarantees loans for eligible clean energy projects and provides direct loans to eligible manufacturers of advanced technology vehicles and components.

The Office of Procurement and Assistance Management (OPAM) oversees policies and procedures for all DOE contracting, financial assistance, and business-related activities. OPAM's website offers a thorough compendium of links to information on doing business with DOE. Small businesses seeking grants can participate in the Office of Science's Small Business Innovation Research (SBIR) Program and Small Business Technology Transfer (SBTT) Program. The Office of Economic Impact and Diversity works with minority-owned and other small businesses to advance DOE's mission.

Department of Health and Human Services (HHS)

How it can assist AAPIs

HHS is the principal agency for protecting the health of all individuals and providing essential human services. HHS administers more funding opportunities than all other federal agencies combined, with 400 grant programs across 18 agencies. Many HHS-funded programs are provided or administered at the local level by state or county agencies in conjunction with community organizations and the private sector.

HHS is responsible for implementing many components of the Affordable Care Act (ACA), signed into law on March 23, 2010, which gives Americans greater access and control in their health-care choices.

The passage of the ACA enhances HHS' charge to reduce health disparities through the development of offices of Minority Health in six agencies within HHS. The HHS Action Plan to Reduce Health Disparities and the National Stakeholder Strategy for Achieving Health Equity outline goals and actions, as well as public and private sector initiatives, to reduce health disparities among racial and ethnic minorities.

AAPI women between the ages of 15-24 have the highest rates of suicide among women in that age group, and AAPI women over 65 have the highest rates of suicide among all races in that age.

— HHS, Office of Minority Health, Health Status of Asian American and Pacific Islander Women, April 2007.

The Office of Minority Health (OMH) works in partnership with communities and organizations in the public and private sectors to improve the health of racial and ethnic minority populations through development of health policies and programs that will help eliminate health disparities. OMH programs address disease prevention, health promotion, risk reduction, healthier lifestyle choices, use of health-care services, and barriers to health care. OMH also administers grant programs to support community organizations and science-based efforts to eliminate health disparities. Call 1-800-444-6472 for more information.

The National Institute for Minority Health and Health Disparities advises the National Institutes of Health (NIH) on the development of NIH-wide policy issues related to minority and other health disparities research, develops a comprehensive strategic plan governing the conduct and support of this research, and administers funds through grants and through leveraging the programs of the NIH.

The Substance Abuse and Mental Health Services Administration works to reduce the impact of substance abuse and mental illness. SAMHSA's National Network to Eliminate Disparities in Behavioral Health, provides grants to build a national network of diverse racial, ethnic, cultural, and sexual minority communities and organizations to promote policies, practices, standards, and research to eliminate behavioral health disparities.

The following agencies within HHS work on the delivery of health care services.

The Health Resources and Services Administration (HRSA), comprised of six bureaus and 13 offices, is the primary federal agency for improving access to health-care services for people who are uninsured, isolated, or medically vulnerable. The Bureau of Primary Health Care (BPHC) funds health centers in underserved communities that provide access to high-quality, family-oriented, and comprehensive primary and preventive health care for people who are low-income, uninsured, or face other obstacles to getting health care. For funding opportunities, visit http://www.hrsa.gov/grants, and for locating local health centers, visit findahealthcenter.hrsa.gov.

In 2009, HRSA health centers served roughly 19 million Americans, including nearly 500,000 Asian Americans. Nearly two-thirds of Asian Americans served by these health centers had limited English proficiency

— HHS, Health Resources and Services Administration, May 2011.

The Centers for Medicare and Medicaid Services (CMS) administers: Medicare, a health insurance program for people age 65 or older; people under age 65 with certain disabilities; and people of all ages with end-stage renal disease (permanent kidney failure requiring dialysis or a kidney transplant); Medicaid, a state-administered program and available only to certain low-income individuals and families who fit into an eligibility group that is recognized by federal and state law; and the Children's Health Insurance Programs (CHIP), a state and federal partnership that targets uninsured children and pregnant women in families with incomes too high to qualify for most state Medicaid programs, but often too low to afford private coverage. The Center for Consumer Information & Insurance Oversight, within CMS, oversees the implementation of the provisions of the ACA related to private health insurance.

The following agencies within HHS work on prevention measures to protect the public health.

The Centers for Disease Control and Prevention (CDC) protects the public health of the nation by providing leadership and direction in the prevention and control of diseases and other preventable conditions and responding to public health emergencies.

The Division of Viral Hepatitis provides the scientific and programmatic foundation for the prevention, control, and elimination of hepatitis virus infections in the United States, and assists the international public health community in these activities.

The Division of Diabetes Translation translates diabetes research into daily practice to better understand the impact of the disease, influence health outcomes, and improve access to quality health care. The National Diabetes Education Program (NDEP) is a joint effort of CDC and NIH and involves public and private partners in efforts to improve diabetes management and outcomes, promote early diagnoses, and prevent or delay the onset of diabetes in the U.S. and its territories. NDEP resources in AAPI languages are available on its website.

The U.S. Food and Drug Administration (FDA) ensures that human and animal drugs, biological products, and medical devices are safe and effective and that electronic products that emit radiation are safe.

The following agencies within HHS work on human services.

The Administration for Children and Families (ACF) promotes the economic and social well-being of America's most vulnerable populations and communities. ACF's programs (ACF Directory of Program Services) are focused on individuals and families with low income, refugees, people with developmental disabilities, and others.

The Office of Refugee Resettlement oversees and provides guidance to state-administered programs that provide assistance and services to refugee, asylees, certain Amerasian immigrants, Cuban and Haitian entrants, as well as victims of human trafficking.

The Office of Family Assistance administers Temporary Assistance for Needy Families (TANF) programs, time-limited assistance to needy families with children to promote work, responsibility, and self-sufficiency.

The Office of Head Start provides grants to local public and private nonprofits and for-profit agencies to provide comprehensive child development services to economically disadvantaged children and families, and has a special focus on helping preschoolers develop early reading and math skills.

The Child Care and Development Fund provides funding for states to improve the quality of child care and to provide child care assistance for so they can work or attend training or obtain other education. Each state has its own eligibility guidelines. You may apply for child care assistance at a state or local agency.

The Family and Youth Services Bureau provides a number of programs addressing youth and family issues, including programs for runaway and homeless youths, teen pregnancy prevention, and family violence prevention and services. Additionally, the FYSB administers funding from the Family Violence Prevention and Services Act, the primary federal funding stream dedicated to the support of emergency shelter and related assistance for victims of domestic violence and their dependents. The National Clearinghouse on Families & Youth is an information resource that assists current and prospective FYSB grantees, and anyone else who works with at-risk youths and families, to realize their goals, better serve their communities, and improve the lives of young people and their families.

The Office of Community Services provides a range of human and economic development services and activities, intended to ameliorate the causes and characteristics of poverty and otherwise assist persons in need including. Programs include the Community Economic Development Program, the Job Opportunities for Low-Income Individuals, and the Low Income Home Energy Assistance Program.

The Administration on Aging (AoA) is the primary agency designated to carry out the provisions of the *Older Americans Act of 1965*. Programs and services that are administered include: home-delivered meals and other nutrition-related services, transportation, adult day care, legal assistance, and health promotion. AoA's National Family Caregiver Support Program provides grants to states and territories, based on their share of the population aged 70 and over, to fund a range of supports that assist family and informal caregivers to care for their loved ones at home for as long as possible.

Other Resources:

- The Health Finder website and OMH website provide documents created by HHS program offices, printed in English and other Asian and Pacific Island languages. For additional language assistance, contact an information specialist at the OMH Resource Center at: info@minorityhealth.hhs.gov or 1-800-444-6472.

- Information about the HHS grant processes is available here.

- The HHS Grants Forecast provides individuals with advanced notice of upcoming funding opportunities.

Grantee Spotlight: HOPE Clinic; Houston, Texas
Federal Program: Health Center Program; HHS, HRSA

Since 2002, HOPE Clinic, a community health center, has provided comprehensive primary health-care services in a culturally and linguistically related manner to underserved Asian Americans in the Greater Houston, Texas, area, including more than 3,000 Vietnamese American evacuees during Hurricane Katrina. Chief Executive Director Dr. Andrea Caracostis discusses her experience applying for HRSA planning grants and HOPE Clinic's designation to become a Federally Qualified Health Center (FQHC) Look-Alike, which makes it eligible for funding opportunities through HHS.

Establishing a community health center was the vision of a group of Asian American women who established the Asian American Health Coalition (AAHC) in Houston in 1994. AAHC collaborated with another community organization, the Chinese Community Center, to establish HOPE as an all-volunteer part-time health clinic in 2002. HOPE then successfully applied for and received two HRSA planning grants and was designated as a Federally Qualified Health Center Look-Alike.

We used the health center planning grants to conduct a comprehensive community needs assessment, which is a critical component in health center development, in order to fully understand our community's needs to determine meaningful impact. The planning grants were also used to gather essential data and develop detailed business and clinic plans.

HOPE worked on our Look-Alike application for approximately one year before receiving the designation (it actually took three denied applications). Proposal writing was a one-woman operation! The key to the success of the application is about knowing your community and accurately describing your entire population and area; not focusing so much on one specific population or group.

As for technical assistance, our staff took initiative and researched HRSA guidelines. We worked with organizational partners, including the Association of Asian Pacific Community Health Organizations (AAPCHO) and the local Primary Care Association, which provided valuable technical assistance, data, assistance with development of clinic policy and procedures, and provision of operational resources.

My advice to other organizations interested in this program is to take advantage of partnerships, collaborations and outreach, and engage with your community. Use your grant application as your business plan and a check list for your organization. Remember to document and collect baseline data in order to show change and carefully measure your progress to prove success.

For more information on the Health Center Program, visit: http://bphc.hrsa.gov.

Grantee Spotlight: MA`O Organic Farms; Wai`anae, Hawaii
Federal Program: Social and Economic Development Strategies for Native Americans (SEDS) Federal Grant; HHS

MA`O Organic Farms is a fully certified 24-acre organic farm on the highly urbanized island of O`ahu. MA`O offers a variety of community and education programs for youths and adults primarily based on the Wai`anae coast and/or on-site at the farm. MA`O programs all relate to MA`O's mission of land-based community development through growing organic food and supporting youth leaders. Executive Director Kukui Maunakea-Forth explains her experience applying for the SEDS federal grant.

The grant is well-known because the program has a strong history in the Wai`anae community. The goal of the grant is to assist Native communities to achieve the goal of economic and social self-sufficiency. MA`O used the SEDS grant for both economic and social development. The funding helped grow MA`O's youth programs, which develop new young farmers as well as youth leaders equipped to create a regional organic food system in Hawai`i, where food security is a challenge. By developing young farmers and leaders, we ensure that a new generation of people will have jobs and produce food for our community.

We applied for the grant as a start-up, and our primary challenge was developing the organizational capacity to create and submit a competitive proposal. The process was facilitated by HHS' relationship with the community. Though the process was challenging, the experience was rewarding. HHS contracted consultants, who provided technical assistance to the SEDS grant applicants. Local intermediary agencies provided critical input to the process. For instance, one of the agencies, Hawaii Alliance of Community Based Economic Development supports community-based economic development by being a facilitator, catalyst, broker, and producer of training, technical assistance, advocacy, education, and research and development products and services.

My advice for those interested in this program, simply put, is to go for it! In our opinion, the community-centered SEDS grant is one of the most supportive federal grants available. Though many other grants exist, the SEDS grant has fewer levels of the embedded bureaucracy that makes it daunting for smaller, community-oriented projects to administer. At best, you will be successful in obtaining this grant. At worst, you will have gained a valuable learning experience from navigating the process.

For more information on the SEDS grant, visit http://www.acf.hhs.gov/programs/ana.

Department of Homeland Security (DHS)

How it can assist AAPIs

DHS was formed in 2003 and works to build a safe and secure homeland by focusing on the following mission areas: preventing terrorism, securing our borders; enforcing our immigration laws; securing cyberspace; and ensuring resilience to disasters.

U.S. Citizenship And Immigration Services (USCIS) oversees the lawful immigration of individuals to the U.S. and processes such immigration paperwork as petitions for lawful permanent residence (green card applications); citizenship; student, employment, and humanitarian visas; international adoptions; asylum; and other immigration benefits. USCIS services include, immigration forms; Immigration Information Officer appointments at InfoPass, available in English, Vietnamese, Chinese, Tagalog, Korean, and other languages; case status; citizenship applications; Green Card (Permanent Residence) applications; helping family members immigrate to the U.S.; asylum applications; and work authorization applications.

- USCIS Ombudsman provides recommendations for resolving individual and employer issues with USCIS. If you are experiencing problems during the adjudication of an immigration benefit with USCIS you can submit a case problem to the CIS Ombudsman using DHS Form 7001.

U.S. Customs and Border Protection (CBP) is responsible for securing America's borders to protect against threats and prevent the illegal entry of inadmissible persons and contraband, while facilitating lawful travel, trade, and immigration. Each day, CBP welcomes more than 1.1 million international travelers into the U.S. at land, air, and seaports. CBP provides information on traveling to the U.S., including information on the CBP inspection process, traveler entry forms, prohibited items, and other restrictions and policies.

U.S. Immigration and Customs Enforcement (ICE) is responsible for safeguarding homeland security and public safety through the enforcement of federal laws governing border control, customs, trade, and immigration. In addition, ICE Public Engagement seeks to build constructive relationships with community stakeholders through targeted community outreach across the country. The ICE Online Detainee Locator System may be used to locate a detainee who is currently in ICE custody, or who was released from ICE custody within the last 60 days.

The Transportation Security Administration (TSA) is charged with protecting passengers' privacy and facilitating the flow of legitimate commerce. Approximately 48,000 Transportation Security Officers serve in over 450 U.S. airports, where they screen approximately 2 million people a day. TSA's Office of Civil Rights and Liberties reviews concerns about a screening experience where an individual believes he or she was treated differently or discriminated against to ensure that the public are treated in a fair and lawful manner. For information regarding a violation of civil rights or civil liberties while traveling, email TSAExternal-Compliance@dhs.gov, call 1-866-289-9673, or file a civil rights/civil liberties complaint.

The Federal Emergency Management Administration (FEMA) supports the nation's state, local, tribal, territorial, and private partners and first responders. It also improves our capability to prepare for, protect against, respond to, recover from, and mitigate all hazards and natural disasters. Families and individuals that have been impacted by a disaster and need assistance have several options for getting help: look up disaster assistance grants and programs, register online or through a web-enabled mobile device, or call 1-800-621-FEMA (3362) or 1-800-462-7585 (TTY) for the hearing and speech impaired.

The Office for Civil Rights and Civil Liberties (CRCL) advises DHS on ways to promote respect for civil rights and civil liberties in policy creation and implementation; communicates with individuals and communities whose civil rights and civil liberties may be affected by DHS activities, and informs them about policies and avenues of redress. CRCL investigates and resolves civil rights and civil liberties complaints filed by the public regarding DHS policies or activities, or actions taken by DHS personnel, including: discrimination based on race, ethnicity, national origin, religion, gender, or disability; violation of rights while in immigration detention or as a subject of immigration enforcement; discrimination or inappropriate questioning related to entry into the U.S.; or physical abuse or any other type of abuse. Complaint forms can be submitted via mail, email (crcl@dhs.gov), or telephone (1-866-644-8360). Complaints are accepted in languages other than English and may be filed by members of the public, federal agencies or agency personnel, non-governmental organizations, media reports and other sources.

Department of Housing and Urban Development (HUD)

How it can assist AAPIs

HUD works with community organizations focused on housing, homeownership, public services, or community development to ensure that everyone can access HUD's programs and resources. HUD provides individual housing services from housing counseling to rental assistance. Contact a regional or local office in your area to reach HUD.

All HUD grants are managed by the Office of Departmental Grants Management and Oversight. HUD competitive funding opportunities are tailored to help communities design and implement housing, economic development, and community development programs to address local needs.

The Community Development Block Grant (CDBG) Technical Assistance program provides funding for experienced organizations to help CDBG grant recipients to plan, develop, and administer activities under the CDBG program.

Capacity Building for Community Development and Affordable Housing enhances the capacity and ability of community development corporations and community housing development organizations to carry out community development and affordable housing activities that benefit low-income families.

The Fair Housing Initiatives Program is designed to increase the number of referrals to HUD of discriminatory housing practices. Eligible organizations provide fair lending enforcement services or inform and educate the public about their rights and obligations under fair housing laws. Funding is also available to build capacity and establish new fair housing enforcement organizations.

The Housing Counseling Program funds HUD-approved counseling agencies and intermediaries that provide counseling services within their communities. HUD also funds organizations that improve and standardize the quality of counseling by training housing counselors.

Healthy Homes and Lead Hazard Control office improves the efficacy of methods for detecting and controlling housing-related health and safety hazards in the home. Eligible applicants carry out related research studies, demonstrations, or outreach.

The Rural Housing and Economic Development Program funds the development and implementation of innovative housing and economic development activities in rural areas.

HUD funds a range of homeless and targeted housing assistance. Continuum of Care programs award organizations that provide housing and supportive services for the homeless. Supportive Housing for the Elderly and Supportive Housing for Persons with Disabilities provide interest-free capital advances to organizations to construct, rehabilitate, or acquire rental housing with support services for the elderly or persons with disabilities. HUD also funds the Assisted Living Conversion Program for people who are elderly or who have disabilities. In addition, owners of multifamily assisted housing developments are eligible for funds to hire service coordinators and pay associated administrative costs.

The Housing Counseling Program provides grants to HUD-approved housing counseling agencies to provide housing counseling services to homebuyers, homeowners, low- to moderate-income renters, and the homeless. The program's goals are to improve financial literacy, expand homeownership opportunities, improve access to affordable housing and preserve homeownership. The Office of Housing and Office of Public and Indian Housing contributes to building and preserving healthy neighborhoods and communities; maintaining and expanding homeownership, rental housing, and health-care opportunities; stabilizing credit markets in times of economic disruption; and operating with a high degree of public and fiscal accountability.

HUD provides comprehensive information regarding foreclosure, including state and local foreclosure counselors and resources. In addition, HUD and the Department of Treasury developed a helpful tool, available at http://www.makinghomeaffordable.gov. Homeowners can call 1-888-995-HOPE (4673) to speak to an expert advisor immediately, 24 hours a day, seven days a week, 365 days a year, in over 170 languages.

Housing Choice Vouchers are rental subsidies for eligible tenant families and persons. The voucher program also provides a number of development opportunities for public housing organizations. Housing choice vouchers are administered locally by local public housing agencies.

The Office of Fair Housing and Equal Opportunity (FHEO) administers and enforces housing and anti-discrimination federal laws. FHEO investigates over 10,000 housing discrimination complaints annually and helps ensure residents have equal access to the housing of their choice. Anyone who believes they are the victims of housing discrimination can file a complaint by filling out an online complaint form, or calling: 1-800-669-9777 (voice) or 1-800-927-9275 (TTY).

Other Resources:

- The HUD Limited English Proficiency website provides documents created by HUD program offices in 12 different languages. If your organization is interested in using these translated materials, call 202-402-7017.

- For access to research and data sets relating to housing and urban development: http://www.huduser.org.

Department of the Interior (DOI)

How it can assist AAPIs

DOI is uniquely positioned to employ thousands of people to work in the great outdoors, providing Americans with hands-on experience with green career pathways as technicians, scientists, engineers, land managers, and educators, among others professions. DOI protects America's natural resources and heritage, honors our cultures and tribal communities, and supplies the energy to power our future.

DOI bureaus and offices include the following: The Office of Insular Affairs has the administrative responsibility for coordinating federal policy in the territories of American Samoa, Guam, the U.S. Virgin Islands, and the Commonwealth of the Northern Mariana Islands, and oversight of federal programs and funds in the freely associated states of the Federated States of Micronesia, the Republic of the Marshall Islands, and the Republic of Palau. The Office of Native Hawaiian Relations' mission is to serve as a liaison with the Native Hawaiian community and work with the Department and its bureaus on issues affecting Hawaii. The National Park Service manages all national parks, many national monuments, and other conservation and historical properties with various title designations. The U.S. Fish & Wildlife Service works to conserve, protect, and enhance fish, wildlife, plants and their habitats for the continuing benefit of the American people. The U.S. Geological Survey provides impartial information on the health of our ecosystems and environment, the natural hazards that threaten us, the natural resources we rely on, the impacts of climate and land-use change, and the core science systems that help us provide timely, relevant, and useable information.

DOI engages in many types of formal and informal partnership arrangements including: grants, cooperative agreements, and memoranda of understanding. The Office of Small and Disadvantaged Business Utilization provides small and disadvantaged businesses with maximum practicable opportunity to participate in the Interior contracting process, and ensures that small businesses are treated fairly and provided with opportunities to compete and win a fair amount of DOI contracting and subcontracting dollars. The Youth In The Great Outdoors Initiative (Youth GO!) employs, educates, and engages young people from all backgrounds in exploring, connecting with, and preserving America's natural and cultural heritage.

Department of Justice (DOJ)

How it can assist AAPIs

DOJ's mission is to enforce the law and defend the interests of the U.S. according to the law; to ensure public safety against threats foreign and domestic; to provide federal leadership in preventing and controlling crime; to seek just punishment for those guilty of unlawful behavior; and to ensure fair and impartial administration of justice for all Americans. In addition, there are a number of grant programs available to the community.

The Office on Violence Against Women (OVW) provides federal leadership in developing the nation's capacity to reduce violence against women and administer justice for and strengthen services to victims of domestic violence, dating violence, sexual assault, and stalking. OVW administers grants, financial and technical assistance programs to local and state and tribal governments, courts, nonprofit organizations, community-based organizations, institutes of higher education, and state and tribal coalitions across the country that are developing programs, policies, and practices working toward developing more effective responses to violence against women through activities that include direct services, crisis intervention, transitional housing, legal assistance to victims, court improvement, and training for law enforcement and courts. Apply for an OVW grant at: http://www.ovw.usdoj.gov/how-to-apply.html. Some important grants to keep in mind:

- STOP (Services, Training, Officers, and Prosecutors) Violence Against Women Formula Grants to States promotes a coordinated, multidisciplinary approach to enhancing advocacy and improving the criminal justice system's response to violent crimes against women. Ten percent of STOP funding is mandated to develop and support initiatives to address the needs of underserved populations.

- Culturally and Linguistically Specific Services for Victims Program funds projects that promote the maintenance and replication of existing successful domestic violence, dating violence, sexual assault, and stalking community-based programs providing culturally and linguistically specific services and other resources.

- Sexual Assault Services Program (SASP) is the first federal funding stream solely dedicated to the provision of direct intervention and related assistance for victims of sexual assault. SASP encompasses a funding stream for culturally specific organizations and seeks to provide intervention, advocacy, accompaniment, support services, and related assistance for victims, family members, and others affected by sexual assault through direct intervention and related assistance from social service organizations, such as rape crisis centers through 24-hour sexual assault hotlines, crisis intervention, and medical and criminal justice accompaniment.

Executive Office for Immigration Review (EOIR) administers the nation's immigration court system. EOIR primarily decides whether foreign-born individuals, who are charged by the Department of Homeland Security with violating immigration law, should be ordered removed from the U.S. or should be granted relief or protection from removal and be permitted to remain in this country. To make these determinations, EOIR's Office of the Chief Immigration Judge has more than 235 immigration judges who conduct administrative court proceedings, called removal proceedings, in 59 immigration courts nationwide.

Community Relations Service (CRS) provides violence prevention and conflict resolution services for community conflicts and tensions arising from differences of race, color, or national origin. CRS is DOJ's "peacemaker" for these types of community conflicts and tensions. CRS is the only federal agency dedicated to assist state and local units of government, private and public organizations, and community groups with preventing and resolving racial and ethnic tensions, incidents and civil disorders, and in restoring racial stability and harmony.

Since 9/11/2001, DOJ has investigated more than 800 incidents involving violence, threats, vandalism, and arson against persons perceived to be Muslim or to be of Arab, Middle Eastern, or South Asian origin.

—DOJ, *Fact Sheet: Protect the Civil Rights of American Muslims Outreach and Enforcement Efforts*, March 2011.

The Civil Rights Division works to uphold the civil and constitutional rights of all Americans, particularly some of the most vulnerable members of our society. The Division's 11 sections enforce federal statutes prohibiting discrimination on the basis of race, color, sex, disability, religion, familial status and national origin.

The Criminal Section prosecutes cases involving the violent interference with liberties and rights defined in the Constitution or federal law. The rights of both U.S. citizens and noncitizens are protected. Issues addressed by the Criminal Section include hate crimes, misconduct by enforcement officials, **human trafficking**, interference with the exercise of religious beliefs and destruction of religious property, and interference with the right to vote.

The Federal Coordination and Compliance Section coordinates across federal agencies to ensure that they are consistently and effectively enforcing civil rights statutes and related Executive Orders that prohibit discrimination in federally assisted programs and in the federal government's own programs and activities. Among its duties, this section is responsible for ensuring that persons with limited English proficiency are able to meaningfully access federal programs and services for which they are eligible.

The Office of Special Counsel for Immigration-Related Unfair Employment Practices enforces the statute that prohibits discrimination in hiring, firing, or recruitment or referral for a fee that is based on an individual's national origin or citizenship status. The statute also prohibits unfair documentary practices during the employment eligibility verification (Form I-9) process ("document abuse"), and retaliation or intimidation.

The Disability Rights Section works to achieve equal opportunity for people with disabilities in the U.S. by implementing the *Americans with Disabilities Act (ADA)*. Section activities affect 6 million businesses and nonprofit agencies, 80,000 units of state and local government, 49 million people with disabilities, and over 100 federal agencies and commissions in the Executive Branch.

The Educational Opportunities Section enforces statutes and court decisions in a diverse array of cases involving elementary and secondary schools and institutions of higher education to ensure that school officials do not discriminate against students on the basis of sex, national origin, language barrier, religion, or disabilities. These actions also include bullying and harassment issues.

The Housing and Civil Enforcement Section ensures and protects the public's right to access housing free from discrimination, the right to access credit on an equal basis, the right to patronize places of business that provide public accommodations, and the right to practice one's faith free from discrimination.

The Voting Section enforces the *Voting Rights Act* ensures that, throughout the nation, no person shall be denied the right to vote on account of race or color.

The Special Counsel for Religious Discrimination coordinates cases involving religion-based discrimination, and oversees outreach efforts to religious communities. If you feel you have been discriminated against on the basis of religion, but are unsure which section of the civil rights division to contact, or if you have any problems reaching one of the sections listed above, call the special counsel's office at 202- 353-8622 (voice) or 202-514-0716 (TDD).

File a complaint with the Civil Rights Division or contact your local FBI field office to report incidents of: hate crimes; excessive force, or other Constitutional violations by persons acting as law enforcement officials or public officials; human trafficking and involuntary servitude; force, threats, or physical obstruction to interfere with access to reproductive health-care services; force or threats to interfere with the exercise of religious beliefs and destruction, defacing, or damage of religious property; or force or threats to interfere with the right to vote based on race, color, national origin, or religion.

Other Resources:

- http://www.LEP.gov promotes a positive and cooperative understanding of the importance of language access to federally conducted and federally assisted programs. This site also acts as a clearinghouse, providing and linking to information, tools, and technical assistance regarding limited English proficiency and language services for federal agencies, recipients of federal funds, users of federal programs and federally assisted programs, and other stakeholders.

- This chart describes federal funding opportunities that may be available to state and local courts to provide language assistance services to LEP individuals. Each chart includes the name of the federal agency providing the funding, the program name, whether state courts are eligible, whether the funding can be used to provide language assistance services, and the location for more information about the program and past recipients.

Grantee Spotlight: Asian & Pacific Islander Institute on Domestic Violence; San Francisco, Calif.

Federal Program: Culturally and Linguistically Specific Services; OVW, DOJ

The Asian & Pacific Islander Institute on Domestic Violence (API Institute) is a national resource center and a training and technical assistance provider on gender-based violence in Asian, Native Hawaiian and Pacific Islander communities. It serves a national network of advocates, community members, national organizations, service agencies, professionals, researchers, policy advocates, and activists from community and social justice organizations. Its goals are to strengthen culturally relevant advocacy, promote community organizing, and influence public policy and systems change. Director Firoza Chic Dabby explains her experience disseminating information to the API Institute's constituents on a new OVW grant program, Culturally and Linguistically Specific Services (CLSSP).

Our federal grants from HHS and OVW fund us to serve as a Technical Assistance and Training provider. We used this grant from OVW to provide training and technical assistance to our constituents—domestic violence programs serving AAPIs. For many organizations, the application process can be difficult. OVW hosts calls to assist through the process. Working in collaboration with OVW and other Technical Assistance & Training providers is important, as well as paying attention to detail during the application process.

My advice to those interested in this grant program is to: 1) Assess if your organization has the capacity to apply for and administer a federal grant; 2) Follow the necessary steps to register and to get announcements related to the RFP; and 3) Review your program ideas to see how they will be staffed, if they fit your mission, and who you might collaborate with—if collaborating, begin the process early. It is very important to review procedures to determine if your organization is eligible and to ensure it has the basic requirements stated by the federal agency (like a DUNS number) to submit the application. Fiscal management is critical to administering federal grants. Be sure your organization has an accounting system to manage and submit budget reports, and that it has sufficient cash flow to meet grant expenses (federal grants do not make awards at the start of the grant period, but in monthly drawdowns).

For more information on the API Institute, visit http://www.apiidv.org. For information on OVW programs, visit http://www.ovw.usdoj.gov/ovwgrantprograms.htm.

Department of Labor (DOL)

How it can assist AAPIs

DOL promotes the welfare of wage earners, job seekers, and retirees in the U.S. by improving working conditions, advancing employment opportunities and assuring work-related benefits and rights. DOL administers and enforces more than 180 federal laws, which along with the regulations that implement them, cover workplace activities for 10 million employers and 125 million workers. DOL also administers a number of workforce-related programs, services, and grants, some of which are listed below.

The following offices enforce laws and regulations that protect workers in areas of wages paid, hours worked, health and safety, and discrimination. Federal laws also protect specific classes of workers, including children, nonimmigrant foreign workers, farm workers, veterans, and employees of federal contractors.

- The Wage and Hour Division (WHD) is a worker protection agency that enforces federal minimum wage, overtime pay, recordkeeping, and child labor requirements of the *Fair Labor Standards Act*. WHD also enforces the *Family and Medical Leave Act* and the *Migrant and Seasonal Agricultural Worker Protection Act*. The agency is engaged in a number of outreach efforts targeting AAPI communities, such as the Know-Your-Rights Regional Outreach Initiative. Among the programs in this initiative are: Compliance Outreach to the Asian Community and Hispanics (COACH), Rapid Employee Assistance in Chinese Hotline (REACH), Protecting Immigrant Employee with Compliance and Education (PIECE), and The Information Group for Asian American Rights (TIGAAR). Finally, WHD's "We Can Help" campaign focuses on educating vulnerable, low-wage workers about their rights. The campaign includes materials in Chinese, Vietnamese, Korean, Thai, and Spanish, which can be found online or by calling 1-866-487-9243.

- The Occupational Safety and Health Administration (OSHA) was created in 1971 by Congress under the *Occupational Safety and Health Act*, to ensure safe and healthful working conditions for working men and women by setting and enforcing standards and by providing training, outreach, education, and assistance.

    - Workers have a right to receive information and training (in a language they can understand) about hazards, methods to prevent harm, and OSHA standards that apply to their workplace. OSHA offers publications, some in several languages, to help employers and workers prevent injuries and illnesses on the job. Workers can file a complaint, asking OSHA to inspect their workplace if they believe there is a serious hazard or their employer is not following the rules. OSHA law provides workers with the right to exercise their rights under the law without retaliation or discrimination.
    - Employers must follow all relevant OSHA safety and health standards; find and correct hazards; inform employees about chemical hazards through training, alarms, and other methods; and keep accurate records of work-related injuries and illnesses. Visit the OSHA website or call 1-800-321-6742 to submit a workplace safety and health question, find out more information about a hazard, or request an OSHA inspection of a worksite.

- The Employee Benefits and Security Administration (EBSA) educates and assists the 150 million Americans covered by private retirement plans, health plans, and welfare benefit plans, as well as plan sponsors and members of the employee benefits community. EBSA balances proactive enforcement with compliance assistance and works to provide quality assistance to plan participants and beneficiaries. EBSA administers and enforces the *Employee Retirement Income Security Act*, which sets minimum standards for voluntarily established retirement and health plans in private industry to provide protection for individuals in these plans. EBSA assists participants who inquire about their rights under the law and helps to resolve disputes they are encountering with their plan. EBSA has responded to inquiries in Mandarin, Cantonese, Vietnamese, Korean, Lao, Tagalog, Thai, Hindi, Cambodian, and Bengali languages. To further assist the AAPI community, EBSA has created a publication to assist dislocated workers in Chinese, Korean, Vietnamese, and Lao. More information on EBSA's activities and the resources that we have available for retirement and health plan participants can be found at the website or by calling 1-866-444-3272.

- The Office of Federal Contract Compliance Programs (OFCCP) holds those who do business with taxpayer dollars, over 200,000 federal contractors and subcontractors, to the fair and reasonable standard that they take affirmative action and prohibit discrimination on the bases of gender, race, color, national origin, religion, disability, and status as a protected veteran. Anyone who is employed by or tries to get a job with those companies (nearly one in four American workers) is protected by OFCCP's legal authorities. The agency regularly audits contractors to make sure they have fair practices when it comes to how they hire, fire, place, pay, and promote their workers. If you feel that you, or someone you know, may have been the victim of discrimination by a company that contracts with the government, or if you are a business in need of assistance on how to comply with the laws we enforce, please see the OFCCP website or call 1-800-397-6251.

The mission of the Employment and Training Administration (ETA) is to contribute to the more efficient functioning of the U.S. labor market by enhancing employment opportunities and promoting business prosperity by administering high-quality job training, employment, labor market information, and income maintenance services primarily through state and local workforce development systems. The Public Workforce System operates through ETA's *Workforce Investment Act* formula funding to state workforce agencies, a network of approximately 3,000 One-Stop Career Centers nationwide that provide job seekers and employers with a range of employment and training services, including tools for career exploration, staff recruitment, understanding salary and benefits, job search assistance, resume building, and interview strategies.

- Information on the nearest One-Stop Career Center in your area can be found at: http://www.careeronestop.org.

- For online employment law assistance for workers and small businesses, visit http://www.dol.gov/elaws.

In addition to the public workforce system, grant opportunities are available through ETA, which awards competitive funding to support a variety of priorities in employment and training programming and services. These opportunities are announced through Solicitations for Grant Applications, published in the *Federal Register*, on ETA's Grants and Contracts website, and at http://www.grants.gov.

Grantee Spotlight: Asian Immigrant Women Advocates (AIWA); Oakland, Calif.
Federal Program: Susan Harwood Training Grant (SHTG); OSHA

AIWA is a community organization that works with women workers employed in the garment, hotel, restaurant, electronics assembly, and other low-wage industries in the San Francisco Bay Area. AIWA's mission is to empower low-income, limited English speaking Asian immigrant women through education, leadership development, and collective action, so that they can improve their working and living conditions. Executive Director Young Shin explains her experience applying for the SHTG.

A local congressman's office informed us of this grant. When we found out that ergonomics was one of the selected training topic areas of SHTG, and special consideration would be given to hard-to-reach and non/limited English speaking workers, we thought that AIWA was well qualified to apply for the grant.

In order to prevent workplace injuries for low-wage immigrant women workers, AIWA proposed to conduct general and industry-specific ergonomic training to Asian immigrant women working in garment and electronic assembly, food services, packaging, and home health care, a workforce that suffers from repetitive stress and other musculoskeletal injuries, and is typically not reached by English language trainings.

Although AIWA had previously received a number of federal and state grants, we had to learn and familiarize ourselves with the terms and requirements of the SHTG application and process. We registered with Grants.gov, *reviewed the grant opportunity announcement, and started identifying former SHTG grantees and AIWA allies and supporters who were familiar with SHTG to understand and assess what it takes to be a successful applicant.*

DOL-OSHA provided two staff, a program analyst and the director of Office of Training and Educational Programs, to answer questions about the application process via emails and calls. Staff members from the University of California, Berkeley's Labor Occupational Health Program; an SHTG grantee; and staff from Cal OSHA, the California Department of Public Health Services, as well as another organization, Asian Community Mental Health Services, all assisted us with the grant process and application.

My advice to others who are interested in this grant: Identify previous grantees that are similar to your organization and/or whose staff members you can ask about the grant. Learn from them about the process and other relevant issues. Identify your friends, allies, and supporters who are familiar with the grant. Ask them to write or identify others who can support your proposal by writing support letters and making phone calls. Find someone who has experience in writing a federal grant and ask him/her to provide technical assistance. Ask and clarify with SHTG staff any questions you might have via emails or phone calls. It's technical, but nonetheless very important: submit the proposal at least two days before the deadline so you don't miss the deadline!

For more information on the SHTG, visit: http://www.osha.gov/dte/sharwood/index.html.

Department of the Treasury ("Treasury")

How it can assist AAPIs

Treasury plays a vital role in providing financial resources to increase AAPI economic opportunities and promote community development investments. Through the Community Development Financial Institutions (CDFI) Fund, Treasury has helped AAPIs receive credit, capital, and financial services that they otherwise might not have had access to. Treasury also provides resources to improve financial literacy and financial access for every American to help ensure that families' financial futures are more secure.

The Community Development Financial Institutions Fund offers responsible loan products and technical assistance to underserved populations to promote economic revitalization and community development. The CDFI Fund supports small businesses, minority entrepreneurs, and businesses located in underserved urban, rural, and reservation communities. CDFIs play a vital role in serving low-income communities that are often considered too risky by mainstream financial institutions.

CDFI Fund awardees serving AAPI communities have received awards to renovate and develop affordable housing units, provide financing to first-time homebuyers, and help open Individual Development Accounts and new accounts for AAPIs.

— Community Development Financial Institutions Fund, Treasury, *Financial Services Provided by Community Development Financial Institutions in AAPI Communities*, February 2011.

Community Development Financial Institutions (CDFI) Program is a competitive award program through which financial and technical assistance awards are made to build the capacity of CDFIs.

The Native Initiatives program helps increase the number and capacity of Native CDFIs to overcome barriers to financial services in Native communities. There are six CDFIs dedicated to serving Native Hawaiian communities.

New Markets Tax Credit Program attracts investment capital to low-income communities by permitting individual and corporate investors to receive a tax credit against federal income taxes in exchange for making equity investments in specialized financial institutions called Community Development Entities.

Bank Enterprise Awards Program incentivizes FDIC-insured financial institutions to expand investments in CDFIs and to increase lending, investment, and service activities within economically distressed communities.

CDFI Bond Guarantee Program supports CDFI lending and investment activity by providing a source of long-term, patient capital through a bond that can be sold in capital markets. It is a federally guaranteed CDFI bond for community and economic development.

Financial education and financial access efforts strive to improve financial education and provide Americans with greater access to the tools and resources needed to make smart financial decisions. Through programs, grants, and other assistance, Treasury advances the financial capabilities of the public.

The Community Financial Access Program (CFAP) increases low- and moderate-income families' and individuals' access to financial services and financial education. The program helps communities build sustainable approaches to expand financial access among community residents.

The Financial Literacy and Education Commission provides a number of resources for national financial education through http://www.mymoney.gov. Covering a wide spectrum of topics ranging from mortgages to consumer rights, the website is a tool for financial strategy and success.

Treasury Grant Program for Financial Education and Counseling awards grants to organizations to enable them to provide a range of financial education and counseling services to prospective homebuyers. These services must increase financial knowledge, improve financial strategizing and decision-making capabilities of prospective homebuyers, help prospective homebuyers improve their credit scores through a greater understanding of the credit system, or educate prospective homebuyers about short-term and long-term saving options. For more information on the Financial Education and Counseling Program, email cdfihelp@cdfi.treas.gov or call 202-622-6355.

Treasury offers strategies and resources for developing your own spending plan, as well as resources on learning how to protect your consumer rights, and accessing financial information.

Grantee Spotlight: Asian Human Services (AHS); Chicago, Ill.
Federal Program: Community Development Financial Institutions (CDFI); Treasury

AHS is the Midwest's largest Pan-Asian health and human services agency, and provides a wide range of services to low-income, at-risk members of the community. Among its many services, which are offered in more than 28 languages, is an adult education program that includes English as a Second Language classes and basic computer training. AHS Chief Executive Officer Abha Pandya describes her experience applying for a loan from a CDFI.

AHS was looking to acquire a new building for its adult education program and found a local Chicago CDFI, the Illinois Facilities Fund (IFF), which provided real estate consulting services and below-market-rate real estate and equipment loans for nonprofits serving low-income and special-needs communities. With the CDFI funding, AHS was able to acquire a new building for its adult education program. The new AHS facility, which opened in July 2008, provided space for classes, computer training, and even a child care center for the children of parents attending classes. AHS' loan from IFF allowed us to expand its capabilities in serving the Asian, immigrant, and refugee communities that need the most help. Without IFF a lot of things we have done could not have been possible—we also worked with IFF on the acquisition of two other buildings for education and child care purposes. During the application process, IFF conducted a building and cost assessment of the facility that we were interested in acquiring before offering us a loan. IFF was very consultative, very supportive, and gave us a lot of guidance throughout the application process.

For more information on the CDFI Fund, visit http://www.cdfifund.gov.

Department of Veterans Affairs (VA)

How it can assist AAPIs

VA strives to provide veterans with benefits and services with the highest standards of compassion, commitment, excellence, professionalism, integrity, accountability, and stewardship. With the ongoing conflicts in Afghanistan and Iraq, and the aging veteran population, VA plays a critical role in providing AAPI veterans and their families with benefits and pertinent information.

VA provides a Medical Benefits Package to enrolled veterans. This comprehensive plan provides a full range of outpatient and inpatient services within the VA health-care system. Veterans may apply for enrollment online, by mail, in person, or by phone, and may obtain more health benefits information by calling 1-877-222-8387 (1-877-222-VETS). VA applies a variety of factors in determining eligibility for enrollment. Once a veteran is enrolled, health-care services are provided at any of the over 1,400 medical centers and clinics across the country. VA's comprehensive medical benefits package includes a full range of mental health services, including screening and treatment for Post-Traumatic Stress Disorder (PTSD) and Traumatic Brain Injury (TBI). VA's Readjustment Counseling program provides free counseling and related services to combat veterans in Vet Combat Call Centers located across the country.

Veterans' benefits include disability compensation, pensions, education, home loans, life insurance, vocational rehabilitation, survivors' benefits, medical benefits, and burial benefit. The Post 9/11 GI Bill provides financial support for education and housing to individuals with at least 90 days of aggregate service on or after Sept. 11, 2001, or to individuals discharged with a service-connected disability after 30 days. The VA Home Loan Program assists veterans with financing the purchase of homes with favorable loan terms and at a rate of interest that is usually lower than the rate charged on other types of mortgage loans. Burial and Memorial Benefits provide burial space for veterans and their eligible family members. For more information or to confirm eligibility, contact the nearest VA regional office at 1-800-827-1000. The Office of Small and Disadvantage Business Utilization (OSDBU) assists Service-Disabled Veteran-Owned Small Businesses, Veteran Owned Small Businesses, Small Disadvantaged Businesses, HUBZone Businesses, and Women-Owned Small Businesses with identifying VA contract opportunities. OSDBU provides outreach and liaison support to business (small and large) and other members of the public and private sectors concerning small business acquisition issues. VA Disability Compensation applies to veterans with service-related disabilities and who were discharged under other than dishonorable conditions. The Vocational Rehabilitation and Employment VetSuccess Program assists veterans with service-connected disabilities to prepare for, find, and keep suitable jobs, or to improve their ability to live as independently as possible. VA Life Insurance programs were developed to provide insurance benefits for veterans and service members who may not be able to get insurance from private companies because of the extra risks involved in military service or a service-connected disability.

Other Resources:

- Comprehensive information on all VA benefits, and benefits available to veterans from other agencies, may be found at: http://www.va.gov.

- The Center for Minority Veterans assists eligible veterans in their efforts to receive benefits and services from VA. The Center is dedicated to ensuring that all veterans are aware of benefits, services, and programs offered by VA.

- Additional state and local resources are available through State Veteran Affairs offices and Veterans Service Organizations.

- Find the nearest location for VA hospitals and clinics, Vet Centers, Regional Benefits Offices, Regional Loan Centers, and cemeteries.

additional federal agencies

Corporation for National & Community Service (CNCS)

How it can assist AAPIs

CNCS is a federal agency that engages more than 5 million Americans in service through its Senior Corps, AmeriCorps, and Learn and Serve America programs, and leads President Obama's national call to service initiative, *United We Serve*. CNCS participants serve through more than 70,000 organizations that use national service to develop innovative solutions to our nation's most pressing problems. For more information, visit http://www.nationalservice.gov.

CNCS has a clear road map for using national service to address six major challenges facing communities: disaster services, economic opportunity, education, environmental stewardship, healthy futures, and veterans and military families. Below are some of CNCS' programs:

AmeriCorps provides an opportunity for 80,000 adult members of all ages and backgrounds to serve through a network of partnerships with nonprofit organizations, state and local agencies, faith-based and community organizations. AmeriCorps members address critical needs in communities all across America. AmeriCorps is made up of three main programs:

⬛ AmeriCorps State and National: The largest branch of AmeriCorps provides grants to support a broad range of local service programs that engage thousands of Americans in full- or part-time direct service or capacity-building activities to meet critical community needs. AmeriCorps National includes grant opportunities in seven different areas.

⬛ AmeriCorps VISTA: Provides full-time members to community organizations and public agencies to create and expand programs that build capacity for ultimately bringing low-income individuals and communities out of poverty.

⬛ AmeriCorps NCCC: A full-time residential program individuals, age 18–24, that strengthens communities while developing leaders through direct, team-based national and community service.

Senior Corps connects individuals, age 55 and over, with the people and organizations that can use them the most. Volunteers become mentors, coaches, or companions to people in need, or volunteers contribute their job skills and expertise to community projects and organizations. The Foster Grandparent Program connects seniors with children and young people with exceptional needs. The Senior Companion Program brings together seniors with adults in their community who have difficulty with the simple tasks of day-to-day living. RSVP offers "one-stop shopping" for all seniors who want to find challenging, rewarding, and significant service opportunities in their local communities.

Application processes for organizational hosts for AmeriCorps State and National are as follows: AmeriCorps National grants are made directly by CNCS to national nonprofit organizations that operate in two or more states; Indian tribes; and consortia formed across two or more states consisting of institutions of higher education, or other nonprofits, including labor, faith-based and other community organizations. AmeriCorps State works with governor-appointed State Service Commissions to provide grants to organizations seeking AmeriCorps funding to operate a program within only one state. State Service Commissions select which applications to fund or to forward to compete in a national pool.

For individuals, all AmeriCorps programs are open to U.S. citizens or lawful permanent residents. To find the best fit for your skills, interests, and circumstances, check out the online interactive program selector. Benefits: Full-time AmeriCorps members who complete their service earn a Segal AmeriCorps Education Award to help pay for college, graduate school, or to help pay back qualified student loans; members who serve part-time receive a partial award. Some AmeriCorps members may also receive a modest living allowance during their term of service.

Individuals, age 55 and older, are eligible to join three different Senior Corps programs. In the Foster Grandparent and Senior Companion programs, individuals with incomes at or below 200 percent of the poverty line are eligible to receive a tax-free hourly stipend to help offset the cost of volunteering. Nonprofit organizations and state and local agencies can apply for grants to place older adult volunteers in service opportunities to help meet their core missions.

Application Process: Individuals can visit http://www.getinvolved.gov to look for opportunities available in your community, and organizations can visit the website for grant opportunities. Benefits: Senior Corps volunteers help their community, make a difference, save money for the organizations they serve, and add to the quality and health of their lives through service. The Foster Grandparent and Senior Companion programs offer modest stipends and other ways to help offset the costs of your involvement. Other benefits include training and insurance.

Other Resources: To find additional opportunities, including those that do not require a long-term commitment, visit Serve.gov. Visit http://www.nationalservice.gov for more information about CNCS, including:

- The Social Innovation Fund promotes public and private investments in effective nonprofit organizations to help such organizations replicate and expand to serve more low-income communities.

- The Volunteer Generation Fund strengthens the nation's civic infrastructure by helping nonprofits recruit, manage, and support more volunteers.

- The Resource Center provides training and resources to national service programs and nonprofits seeking to expand their capacity and impact.

Environmental Protection Agency (EPA)

How it can assist AAPIs

The mission of EPA is to protect human health and the environment. EPA funds a wide variety of projects to support its mission including environmental justice programs, educational and clean-up efforts, and projects to empower community partnerships and solve local environmental problems. EPA also informs the public about its activities and provides information on a wide range of environmental issues through written materials on its website.

Grant programs help the EPA accomplish its mission of protecting the environment and public health. Funds for a wide range of environmental issues are offered through grant programs and cooperative agreements. Eligibility, deadlines, and award amounts vary by program, and some information on specific programs can be found here. Additionally, there are 10 regional offices that provide information for those seeking funding opportunities in the states within the each region.

- Community Action for a Renewed Environment (CARE) is a competitive grant program that offers an innovative way for a community to organize and take action to reduce toxic pollution in its local environment. Through CARE, a community creates a partnership among organizations that implements solutions to reduce releases of toxic pollutants and minimize people's exposure to them. By providing financial and technical assistance, EPA helps CARE communities get on the path to a renewed environment. The CARE grant program supports and empowers community partnerships that work locally to identify their environmental risks and determine and implement long-term solutions. For more information contact the CARE program at 202-343-9213.

- The Environmental Justice Small Grants Program provides financial assistance to eligible organizations to build collaborative partnerships, to identify the local environmental and/or public health issues, and to envision solutions and empower communities through education, training, and outreach. Successful collaborative partnerships involve not only well-designed strategic plans that build, maintain, and sustain partnerships, but also work towards addressing local environmental and public health issues. For more information contact the Office of Environmental Justice at 202-564-2515.

- The Brownfields Program provides various types of competitive grants funding, in areas that include brownfields assessment, brownfields cleanup, and brownfields revolving loan fund grants. Additionally the program provides environmental workforce development and job-training grants. Brownfields Cleanup grants provide funding for a grant recipient to carry out cleanup activities at brownfield sites. Brownfields assessment grants provide funding for a grant recipient to inventory, characterize, assess, and conduct planning and community involvement related to brownfield sites. Brownfields revolving loan fund grants enable states, political subdivisions, and Indian tribes to make low-interest loans to carry out cleanup activities at brownfields properties. Environmental Workforce Development and Job Training Grants are designed to provide funding to eligible entities, including nonprofit organizations, to recruit, train, and place predominantly low-income and minority, unemployed and underemployed residents of solid and hazardous waste-impacted communities with the skills needed to secure full-time, sustainable employment in the environmental field and in the assessment and cleanup work taking place in their communities. For questions on the workforce development program, contact EPA at 202-566-2772.

- A Superfund Technical Assistance Grant (TAG) provides funds for activities that help communities participate more fully in decision making at eligible Superfund sites. Initial grants may be available to qualified community groups to contract with independent technical advisors to interpret and help the community understand technical information about their site.

- The Office of Environmental Education awards grants each year for educational projects across the country that promote environmental stewardship and help develop knowledgeable and responsible students, teachers, and citizens. This grant program provides financial support for innovative environmental education projects conducted by state and local environmental and education agencies, 501(c)(3) nonprofits, noncommercial broadcasting entities, and tribal schools and nonprofits that design, demonstrate, or disseminate environmental education practices, methods, or techniques as described each year in the solicitation notice.

- The Source Reduction Assistance grant program supports environmental projects that reduce or eliminate pollution at the source. The request for proposals in fiscal year 2011 encouraged proposals for: greenhouse gas reduction, toxic and hazardous materials reduction, resource conservation, efficient business practices, and pollution prevention integration activities. Eligible grantees include states, territories, local governments, city or township governments, independent school districts, incorporated nonprofit organizations (other than institutions of higher education), public and private institutions of higher education, community-based grassroots organizations, and Indian tribes and intertribal consortia.

▧ Solid Waste Management Assistance grant program promotes the use of integrated solid waste management systems to solve solid waste generation and management problems at the local, regional, and national levels. The program seeks to establish and develop partnerships with states, local governments, and nonprofit organizations to assist them in advancing their waste management programs, and to develop and provide education, training, and outreach materials to educate and inform Americans about waste's impact on resource and energy use and pollution. For more information, contact the Office of Resource Conservation and Recovery at 703-308-8460.

Other Resources:

▧ EPA's website is available in Chinese (traditional), Chinese (simplified), Vietnamese, and Korean.

▧ Learn how to live green here.

▧ Stay informed about environmental issues here.

Spotlight Grantee: International District Housing Alliance; Seattle, Wash.
Federal Program: CARE Grant Program; EPA

The Chinatown-International District is one of the oldest cultural centers for Seattle's AAPI population, and its low-income, minority residents are disproportionately affected by environmental pollutants and poor air quality. With the help of a CARE cooperative agreement, the International District Housing Alliance (IDHA) established the International District CARE Project in Seattle's Chinatown-International District. Former IDHA staff member Joyce Pisnanont describes her experience applying for a CARE grant.

IDHA was a recipient of both Level I and Level II grants (see Community Action for a Renewed Environment). IDHA found out about the opportunity from Seattle Public Utilities in 2005, through what is now known as its Environmental Justice and Services Equity division. This grant opportunity appealed to us because of its framework for empowering communities to identify and develop strategies for addressing location-specific environmental justice concerns. This framework was focused on building community capacity and allowed for flexibility and creativity—both of which are important for engaging low-income communities of color and, in particular, multiple generations of stakeholders.

As a small grassroots organization, with little experience in applying for federal grants, and limited knowledge of the technical language used in grant applications, the process was a bit scary at first. For our Level I grant application, we had the help of a professional grant writer to develop a framework for the grant and edit drafts we had written. By the time IDHA became eligible to apply for a CARE Level II, we were much better prepared. We wrote the grant ourselves, but used the same grant writer to proofread and critique the application before submittal. Seattle Public Utilities' Environmental Justice and Services Equity Division was a key player in helping to shape the application.

Public Health—Seattle King County and the University of Washington assisted with Level I grant development. Public Health—Seattle Public Utilities, and local community-based organizations assisted with the Level II application.

My advice to organizations interested in this program is to indicate clear support from the community and local decision makers. Make sure that outcomes are clear and reasonable for your organization to achieve. If you involve youths as a key component of your project, be sure there is capacity and buy-in from participating youth service organizations.

For more information on the CARE Grant, visit http://www.epa.gov/care.

Equal Employment Opportunity Commission (EEOC)

How it can assist AAPIs

The EEOC, an independent federal agency, enforces federal laws that make it illegal to discriminate against a job applicant or employee. Federal laws prohibit discrimination by private and public employers, employment agencies, and labor organizations in all aspects of employment from recruitment to retirement.

Types of discrimination prohibited by federal law include discrimination based on a person's race (including characteristics associated with race, such as hair texture, skin color, or certain facial features), color, religion (in certain instances, employers must also reasonably accommodate an employee's religious beliefs or practices), sex (including pregnancy, sexual harassment, and entitlement to equal pay/compensation), national origin, age, disability, or genetic information. Federal laws also make it illegal to retaliate against an individual who complains about discrimination, files a charge of discrimination, or participates in an employment discrimination investigation or lawsuit.

Individuals may file a charge of employment discrimination at the EEOC office closest to where the individual resides, or at any one of the EEOC's 53 field offices. By telephone: Call 1-800-669-4000 to submit basic information about a possible charge, and EEOC will forward the information to the local field office in your area. Individuals may file a charge by mail to the EEOC consisting of a signed letter identifying the parties and a short description of the events believed to be discriminatory. Note: Federal employees have a different complaint process.

Other Resources:

- EEOC's website provides a compilation of informational documents in Arabic, Chinese, Haitian Creole, Korean, Russian, and Vietnamese.

The American Recovery and Reinvestment Act of 2009 and the Small Business Jobs Act of 2010 have put over 10,000 loans into the hands of Asian American-owned small businesses.

— SBA, March 2011.

Small Business Administration (SBA)

How it can assist AAPIs

Small businesses account for nearly *two out of three new jobs* created today. The SBA is an independent agency of the federal government charged with helping entrepreneurs start, build, and grow businesses. SBA provides counseling and assistance to small businesses to maintain and strengthen the overall economy of the nation. SBA also makes funds available to nonprofit organizations to serve as intermediary lenders through its Microloan Program. Through an extensive network of field offices and partnerships with public and private organizations, SBA delivers its services to people throughout the U.S., Puerto Rico, the U. S. Virgin Islands, and Guam.

To start, manage, and grow a business, SBA offers a variety of free online trainings, podcasts, and documents that cover many business topics for small business owners and those interested in starting a business, available at http://www.sba.gov. These self-paced, easy-to-use tutorials cover a variety of business basics, including how to start an online business, how to write a business plan, how to franchise, and how to adopt technology for business benefits. In addition to online resources, SBA provides small business counseling, mentoring and training to help small businesses grow through a variety of programs and resource partners, located throughout the country, including:

- Small Business Development Centers, a network of roughly 1,000 service centers working as partnerships primarily between the government and colleges and universities, which provide educational services for small business owners and aspiring entrepreneurs.

- Women's Business Centers, a national network of over 100 educational centers providing technical assistance, comprehensive training, and counseling on a vast array of topics in many languages designed to help women start and grow their own businesses.

- Veterans Business Outreach Centers, in 16 locations throughout the U.S., provide entrepreneurial development services, such as business training, counseling and mentoring, and referrals for eligible veterans owning or considering starting a small business.

- Procurement Technical Assistance Centers (PTACs), of which there are 93 nationwide, designed to provide local, in-person counseling and training services to businesses that want to sell products and services to federal, state, and/or local governments.

- SCORE, a nonprofit association of 11,500 volunteer business counselors available online and in local offices throughout the U.S. and its territories, trained to serve as counselors, advisors, and mentors to aspiring entrepreneurs and business owners at no fee, as a community service.

SBA provides a number of financial assistance programs for small businesses that have been specifically designed to meet key financing needs, including debt financing, surety bonds, and equity financing. SBA can help facilitate a loan for small businesses with a third-party lender, guarantee a bond, or help businesses find venture capital. These programs are not direct loans to small businesses. Rather, SBA sets the guidelines for loans, which are then made by its partners (lenders, community development organizations, and microlending institutions). The SBA provides guarantees on most of these loans, thus eliminating much of the risk to the lending partners.

- The Microloan Program: SBA makes funds available to nonprofit community-based organizations as specially designated intermediary lenders. These intermediaries make small, short-term loans to small business concerns and certain types of not-for-profit child care centers.

Federal, state, and local governments offer a wide range of financing programs to help small businesses start and grow their operations. These programs include low-interest loans, venture capital, and scientific and economic development grants. Use the Loans and Grants Search Tool to get a list of financing programs for which small business owners and those interested in starting a business may qualify, and learn more about small business financing programs for research and construction grants.

Federal, state, and local governments offer businesses the opportunity to sell billions of dollars worth of products and services. Many require that some percentage of their procurements be set aside for small businesses. Registering a business with the government is required before bidding on federal government contracts (nearly $100 billion of federal contracts go to small businesses every year). However, businesses can take advantage of several programs designed especially to promote small businesses. The following are examples.

- The SBA 8(a) Business Development Program offers a broad scope of assistance to firms that are owned and controlled at least 51 percent by socially and economically disadvantaged entrepreneurs to gain access to the economic mainstream of American society. The programs help thousands of aspiring entrepreneurs to gain a foothold in government contracting.

- The Women-Owned Small Business Federal Contract Program authorizes contracting officers to set aside certain federal contracts for eligible firms, which are at least 51 percent owned and controlled by one or more women, and primarily managed by one or more women.
- The Historically Underutilized Business Zones (HUBZone) program helps small businesses in urban and rural communities gain increased access to federal procurement opportunities. Small businesses may be eligible for HUBZone certification by employing staff who live in a HUBZone and maintaining a principal office in one of these specially designated areas.
- Energy-Efficient Companies: Various laws, executive orders and procurement regulations now require federal agencies to purchase green (bio-based, recycled content, and energy efficient) products.

Other Resources:

- Find your local SBA office or call the SBA Answer Desk: 1-800-U-ASK-SBA (1-800-827-5722).

- http://www.sba.gov may be translated into multiple languages by clicking on "Translate" in the top right corner.

- USASpending.gov is your source for information about government spending through contracts awarded by the U.S. government.

- The largest governmentwide contracts are established by the U.S. General Services Administration under its GSA Schedules program. Vendors interested in becoming GSA Schedule contractors should review the Getting on the GSA Schedules page.

Social Security Administration (SSA)

How it can assist AAPIs

The SSA is an independent agency of the federal government that administers Social Security, which encompasses several social welfare and social insurance programs for the elderly, families, disabled persons, and survivors.

SSA issues Social Security Numbers (SSNs), which are required to get a job, collect Social Security benefits, and receive other government services. Visit the website to apply for an SSN or to find more information.

- Disability benefits are paid to people who cannot work because they have a medical condition expected to last at least one year or result in death. While some federal programs give money to people with partial disabilities or short-term disabilities, Social Security does not. In general, to get disability benefits, you must meet two different earnings tests: a "recent work" test regarding how much time you worked prior to becoming disabled, which is based on your age at the time you became disabled, and a "duration of work" test to show that you worked long enough to qualify under Social Security.

- Retirement benefits are the foundation on which you can build a secure retirement. The program bases retirement benefit calculations on your earnings during a lifetime of work under the Social Security system. For most current and future retirees, Social Security will base its payments on an average of your 35 highest years of earnings.

- Supplemental Security Income (SSI) is designed to help aged, blind, and disabled people, who have little or no income and few resources. SSI provides cash to meet basic needs for food, clothing, and shelter. The program also pays benefits to disabled children. Many people who are eligible for SSI also may be entitled to receive Social Security benefits.

- Survivor's benefits are Social Security benefits that may be available if you are the survivor of a spouse or child of a worker who died who worked long enough under Social Security to qualify for benefits.

- Medicare is the U.S. health insurance program for people age 65 or older, but certain younger people also can qualify. See page 11, the Department of Health and Human Services for more information.

SSA provides free interpreter services in languages, including Vietnamese, Tagalog, Laotian, Korean, Japanese, Hmong, Chinese, and Cambodian, to help you conduct your Social Security business. You can reach interpreters by calling 1-800-772-1213 or by visiting your local Social Security office.

Business Services Online (BSO) enables organizations and authorized individuals to conduct business with and submit confidential information to Social Security. You must register to use this resource. Registered users may request, activate and access various BSO services and functions, such as verifying employee SSNs.

Other Resources:

- SSA's website provides information in Arabic, Chinese, Korean, Tagalog, Vietnamese, and other languages.

conclusion

The White House Initiative on AAPIs engaged with thousands of diverse stakeholders in cities and towns across the country on how the federal agencies may better meet the needs of the growing AAPI population. Of all the issues that were raised—from the need to collect and analyze data across ethnic subgroups, to disparities in educational attainment and health outcomes in the AAPI community—one issue emerged time and time again: the need to help build the capacity of community-based organizations, coupled with the general lack of awareness of what services and resources the federal government offers to improve the quality of life of AAPIs. During these conversations with community members, the seeds of this *Guide to Federal Agency Resources* were planted. We hope this guide provides individuals and organizations with a starting point and ideas on how to access federal resources available to help improve the quality of life of AAPIs.

Spotlight Grantee: Pacific American Foundation; Kailua, Hawaii
Federal Program: CARE Grant Program: EPA

The Pacific American Foundation (PAF) is a nonprofit organization that plans and administers programs serving Native Hawaiians and Pacific Islanders. PAF found the CARE grant appealing because of the high priority placed on enabling affected communities to empower themselves. With a CARE grant, PAF led the Wai'anae Coast Oahu project to examine the impact of pollutants from human activity on four streams in the area. Human activities, including those producing runoff from agricultural and urban lands adversely affected the subsistence and recreational use of the Wai'anae coastal waters, and the CARE grant enabled extensive data collection to more accurately assess the problem. PAF Executive Director Herb Lee Jr. describes his experience applying for a CARE grant, and shares advice for prospective grantees.

The application process was straightforward, comprehensive, and thought provoking. Support at the EPA Regional level in giving guidance and answering questions was superb. PAF does not have a grant writer on staff and most grants are done in-house or by a contractor with specific skills and experience. EPA was very helpful for both the Level I and Level II application processes.

For those interested in this grant program, do your homework. Start early. Consult with all potential partners early and engage partners and community participants with specific agenda of items to be accomplished. Allow all participants an opportunity to have ownership of the process early. As a result, project outcomes and community solutions will have a much better chance of success.

Treat EPA, or any federal agency, as a true community partner. Create specific expectations for all partners early so everyone knows how to contribute to the final outcome. EPA staff were cooperative and supportive in answering questions we had about the application process, sharing successes in other parts of the country, and really caring about applicants submitting a quality, well-thought-out application. Even though we did not win a grant on our first attempt at a Level II, the process inspired us even more to persevere for the sake of our community and all our motivated partners.

For more information on the CARE Grant, visit http://www.epa.gov/care.